SEQUOYAH

INVENTOR OF WRITTEN CHEROKEE

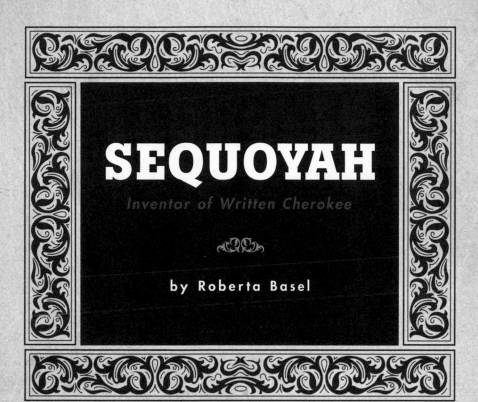

SEQUOYAH

Inventor of Written Cherokee

by Roberta Basel

Content Adviser: Jeffrey Sanders, Ph.D., Associate Professor,
Department of Native American Studies,
Montana State University, Billings

Reading Adviser: Rosemary Palmer, Ph.D.,
Department of Literacy, College of Education,
Boise State University

Compass Point Books ✦ Minneapolis, Minnesota

Compass Point Books
3109 West 50th Street, #115
Minneapolis, MN 55410

Visit Compass Point Books on the Internet at *www.compasspointbooks.com*
or e-mail your request to *custserv@compasspointbooks.com*

Editor: Jennifer VanVoorst
Page Production: Blue Tricycle
Photo Researcher: Lori Bye
Cartographer: XNR Productions, Inc.
Library Consultant: Kathleen Baxter

Art Director: Jaime Martens
Creative Director: Keith Griffin
Editorial Director: Carol Jones
Managing Editor: Catherine Neitge

*To my Grandmother K, a proud Cherokee descendant. With love,
Roberta Jo.*

Library of Congress Cataloging-in-Publication Data
Basel, Roberta.
  Sequoyah : inventor of written Cherokee / by Roberta Basel.
    p. cm. — (Signature lives)
  Includes bibliographical references and index.
  ISBN-13: 978-0-7565-1887-5 (library binding)
  ISBN-10: 0-7565-1887-3 (library binding)
  ISBN-13: 978-0-7565-2197-4 (paperback)
  ISBN-10: 0-7565-2197-1 (paperback)
1. Sequoyah, 1770?–1843—Juvenile literature. 2. Cherokee Indians—
Biography—Juvenile literature. 3. Cherokee language—Writing—Juvenile
literature. 4. Cherokee
language—Alphabet—Juvenile literature. I. Title. II. Series.
  E99.C5.S543 2007
  975.004'975570092—dc22
  [B]   2006027076

Signature Lives

AMERICAN FRONTIER ERA

The young United States was growing at a rapid pace. Settlers were pushing west, conquering and building from coast to coast. World leaders hammered out historic agreements, such as the Louisiana Purchase in 1803, which drastically increased U.S. territory. This westward movement often led to bitter conflicts with Native Americans trying to protect their way of life and their traditional lands. Life on the frontier was often filled with danger and difficulties. The people who wove their way into American history overcame these challenges with a courage and conviction that defined an era and shaped a nation.

KEE   PHŒNIX.

W ECHOTA, THURSDAY FEBRUARY 21, 1828.   NO. 1.

Seguoyah

Table of Contents

1 TALKING LEAVES

ༀༀ

Outside the council house, a lone, middle-aged Cherokee man stood waiting. No one knows what he was thinking, but he must have been excited, nervous, and a little bit worried. At that moment, behind the closed doors of the council house, the past decade of his life's work was being tested, and there was nothing he could do but wait. He knew his success depended upon the mind and hand of his 6-year-old daughter who sat with the Tribal Council inside. Would she be able to remember everything he had taught her? What if she was nervous? What if she was afraid of the powerful men who surrounded her? Would she be able to concentrate and help him pass this important test?

Other people in the Cherokee village must have

The Cherokee National Council awarded Sequoyah a silver medal for his invention.

noticed the man and wondered what was going on. Wasn't he the man they called Sequoyah? People had talked about him for years. Some people said he was a fool. Other people said he was crazy. What was he doing in their village now?

As Sequoyah waited, he probably thought about his past 12 years. At first, he had just been curious.

When Sequoyah first started to work on a writing system, many Cherokee were suspicious of his actions. Some believed he was practicing "bad magic" or some form of witchcraft. Their suspicions could have proved deadly for Sequoyah, for at that time, Cherokee accused of witchcraft could be put to death. Fortunately, Sequoyah was spared— probably because he did not cause trouble. By the time he completed his writing system, most people had come to believe he was simply foolish or crazy— not evil.

He had seen many white men stare at pieces of material no thicker than tree leaves. These leaves seemed to talk to the white men, for after staring at the leaves, the white men knew about people and events in faraway places. Many Cherokee believed these "talking leaves" were magic. They certainly made the white men powerful. Sequoyah, however, did not believe the talking leaves were magic. He told other Cherokee that anyone could write down words, as long as they knew what marks to make. And so, around 1809, Sequoyah had begun to work on figuring out how to make talking leaves that would speak the Cherokee language.

Now, in 1821, Sequoyah was waiting to see if all of his hard

Located in the center of each village, the Cherokee council house was used for important tribal gatherings.

work had paid off. The Tribal Council was giving his daughter Ahyokah a message. She was to write it down using the symbols that Sequoyah had created. Sequoyah knew that she knew his symbols almost as well as he did, but he was likely still a little worried.

Finally, the door to the Tribal Council opened, and Sequoyah was summoned into the room. Ahyokah gave her father a paper filled with his symbols. It was time for Sequoyah to prove that his symbols really held a message. As he looked at the symbols, he spoke the sounds that the symbols represented. He read the message.

The members of the Tribal Council were silent.

Had they heard correctly? Was this some kind of father-daughter trick? Or had Sequoyah really figured out how to make talking leaves that spoke Cherokee?

That day, some members of the Tribal Council realized the importance of what Sequoyah had done. Others still doubted. They wanted more demonstrations to be sure that Sequoyah had not tricked them. More tests were done, and soon, no one could deny it: It was neither witchcraft nor a trick. Sequoyah's talking leaves worked. The Cherokee language could

Today Cherokee and English are both used to direct traffic in Tahlequah, Oklahoma.

indeed be written down.

Sequoyah's invention came at a critical time for the Cherokee. In the face of the encroaching white culture, it helped his people maintain tribal identity by providing them with a way to record, and thus pass on, their traditions. They could communicate across both distance and time. The widespread literacy that resulted also helped all Native Americans by forcing white Americans to reconsider the stereotype of the "savage."

With his invention of a written language, Sequoyah gave his people something that no single person in human history had ever created. And he showed that people of any race or background can achieve great things. ૭

2 A CHEROKEE CHILDHOOD

ꜱꜱꜱ

Before Sequoyah succeeded in writing down the Cherokee language, the Cherokee had an oral tradition but not a written way of recording events. They couldn't write down when people were born or when they married or what happened in their lives. For this reason, historians can only make educated guesses about when Sequoyah was born, and they rely on comments made by other people at that time to figure out other details about Sequoyah's life.

Sequoyah was probably born around 1778 in Tuskegee, near present-day Vonore, Tennessee. The Cherokee lived in the southeastern part of North America. Their land included parts of the present states of Virginia, West Virginia, Kentucky, and South Carolina, as well as western North Carolina, northern

Alabama and Georgia, and eastern Tennessee. They called this area *Sha-cona-ge*, or Land of the Blue Mist, and it covered about 135,000 square miles (351,000 square kilometers). The Cherokee divided their land into four regions: the Overhill Settlements, the Valley Settlements, the Middle Settlements, and the Lower Settlements. Sequoyah grew up in the Overhill Settlements, a series of towns located primarily in eastern Tennessee and so named because travelers needed to cross the mountains to reach them.

Few details are known about Sequoyah's parents. His mother, Wurteh, was a Cherokee woman of the Paint Clan. She came from a well-known family and was related to several prominent Cherokee, including chiefs Old Tassel, Doublehead, and Pumpkinhead.

The Cherokee referred to their homeland as the Land of the Blue Mist.

Much speculation has been made about Sequoyah's father. Most historians believe he was a white man named Nathaniel Gist. Gist was a trader and a friend of General George Washington. He served as a soldier under Washington in the American Revolutionary War and was sent by the general to negotiate with the Cherokee during the conflict. Gist was well-respected by the Native Americans. Chief Old Tassel, Wurteh's brother, said of Gist, "Here is my friend and brother whom I look upon as one of my own people." It was during Gist's time with the Cherokee that Sequoyah was born. Gist, however, was not a part of his son's life. Wurteh raised Sequoyah by herself.

As a child, Sequoyah was a great help to his mother. On their small dairy farm, he washed the milk pails, milked the cows, and strained the milk. When he got older, he built a house over a stream so the milk could be put there to stay cool. Sequoyah also helped with herding the horses

Each Cherokee person belongs to one of seven clans, or groups of people related by a common ancestor. In past times, each clan was responsible for certain tasks. Members of the Wolf Clan were warriors. The Deer Clan people were hunters, while Wild Potato Clan members gathered and taught about plants. Those belonging to the Bird Clan served as messengers, and Long Hair Clan members kept and taught the village's traditions. Members of the Paint Clan were medicine people, while the Blue Clan members were medicine people for children. Clan membership is passed down on the mother's side. Because Sequoyah's mother was a member of the Paint Clan, so was Sequoyah.

and tending the garden and cornfields. He learned to hunt and fish, and in the autumn, he met with traders and exchanged goods for furs.

Like most Cherokee children of the time, Sequoyah did not go to school. There were no Cherokee schools. The only way a Cherokee could get a formal education was to go to one of the white people's schools, but few of the tribe's parents sent their children to those schools. There the children learned only English and the history of white men. They didn't learn anything about their own people

White missionaries established schools in Cherokee territory, but few Cherokee children attended.

or culture. And so, like most Cherokee, Sequoyah stayed at home and learned about his people's way of life. By listening to their stories, he learned lessons about Cherokee traditions, values, beliefs, and history. He also probably took part in tribal celebrations such as the Green Corn Dance, a ritual of thanks for the summer harvest.

Although Sequoyah was raised like most Cherokee children, some things about him set him apart from his people. For one thing, one of his legs was smaller than the other. No one really knows why. Some people say he was born that way. Other people say his leg was injured in a hunting accident, while still others think a childhood illness caused the leg to wither. Whatever the cause may have been, Sequoyah always walked with a limp, and he was unable to participate in the more physically demanding activities of Cherokee life.

Sequoyah's disability played a significant role in his life. In fact, it may have been a factor in determining his Cherokee name. Native American names frequently reflected a personal characteristic, and the name *Sequoyah* is said to be derived from a Cherokee word meaning "pig's foot," a possible reference to his injured leg. Others suggest his name means "sand hill crane," a bird that often stands on one leg.

Because Sequoyah was physically limited, he developed other kinds of skills. At an early age, he was noticed for his artistic ability. He had a gift for drawing and loved to paint pictures of animals. He even made his own brushes and paint. Sequoyah also became well-known for his fine work as a silversmith. He melted French and British coins and used the silver to make jewelry such as earrings, bracelets, and chains. He sometimes used the silver to decorate bridle bits, spurs, and knives.

As his silverwork became better-known, Sequoyah decided that he wanted to stamp his name on his pieces to identify them as his works. But Cherokee was only a spoken language, so "Sequoyah" could not be written down. Fortunately, Sequoyah, like many Cherokee, also had an English name. He was known by most people at the time as George Guess. Some people suggest that he took or was given the name *George* because of George Washington, whom the Cherokee liked and admired. *Guess* was a misspelled version of his father's last name, Gist. An English-educated Cherokee named Charles Hicks showed Sequoyah how to write his English name so he could put it on his silverwork. *George Guess* was the only English he ever learned to write.

Later, other Cherokee began to work with silver, and Sequoyah had to compete for business. He fell on hard times and had a difficult time supporting his mother, who was by then an old woman. He decided instead to become a blacksmith and taught

himself the skills of the trade. He sharpened tools and made and sold axes and hoes and other metal objects. But none of this work would prepare him for what lay ahead. 🐚

Nineteenth-century black-smiths used fire and simple tools to create their products.

3 A Nation Deceived

Chapter

ೲ⚬ೲ

Throughout most of Sequoyah's early years, the Cherokee had trouble with white people and the United States government. Most white Americans believed that all Native Americans, including the Cherokee, were savages and less than human. Existing tensions increased as the growing population of white settlers pushed into lands on which tribes had lived for hundreds of years.

In the late 1700s, the Cherokee tried to gain respect and equality with the whites by giving up their traditional ways and taking on the ways of the white people. The government of the newly formed United States of America promised that if they gave up their hunting lifestyle and became farmers, they would be allowed to keep their homeland. In 1785,

Chief William Weatherford of the Red Stick Creek surrendered to General Andrew Jackson after the Battle of Horseshoe Bend.

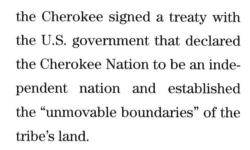

the Cherokee signed a treaty with the U.S. government that declared the Cherokee Nation to be an independent nation and established the "unmovable boundaries" of the tribe's land.

So the Cherokee, once great warriors and hunters, dropped their weapons and became farmers. They built log cabins, mills, churches, and roads. They raised cattle, pigs, cows, chickens, and crops on well-cultivated farms. They even created a government that was very similar to the U.S. government. It had a constitution, a judicial system, and a bicameral legislature. The Cherokee people worked hard at developing their new lives, and by the 1830s, they had become as wealthy and prosperous as their white neighbors.

Although they tried to be more like the whites, many Cherokee quickly learned not to trust the settlers. They had good reasons not to. Despite the Cherokee people's amazing lifestyle transformation, most white people continued to believe that the Cherokee, civilized or not, stood in the way of progress. White settlers ignored the boundaries and pushed into Cherokee land. Many Cherokee responded by moving south. Sequoyah and his mother were among the few who stayed, despite pressure from the whites.

Although he was half white himself, Sequoyah identified himself strongly as a Cherokee and did not trust the white settlers. He watched as time and time again the white men cheated and robbed his people and drove them from their land. He believed whites were "liars, thieves, swindlers, robbers, and all manner of evil doers." Sequoyah did not want his people to become like the white people. He believed they should keep their traditional Cherokee ways. But his distrust of the white people did not stop him from coming to their aid when the United States asked for help.

Native Americans looked on as white settlers traveled past in search of land.

In 1813 and 1814, the United States was fighting a war with a group of Creek Indians called the Red Stick Creek. The Creek were the traditional enemy of the Cherokee, and despite the problems with white intruders, the Cherokee still considered the United States to be an ally. Therefore, when the U.S. government asked the Cherokee for help, many responded. Approximately 200 Cherokee men joined the U.S. forces under the command of Andrew Jackson.

Sequoyah, who was about 35 years old at the time, was among the Cherokee who joined Jackson. He enlisted on October 7, 1813, as a private in the cavalry of Captain John McLamore's company of Mounted and Foot Cherokees. As was required in those days, Sequoyah provided his own horse. He and the other Cherokee soldiers wore the tribe's traditional turban and tunic, deerskin leggings, and moccasins. They also wore white feathers and deer tails on their heads to distinguish themselves from the Creek. The Cherokee carried a variety of weapons, from muskets

*Andrew
Jackson
(1767–1845)*

and rifles to swords, knives, tomahawks, and bows and arrows.

The Cherokee soldiers proved themselves to be a very important part of Jackson's forces when they fought the Red Sticks in March 1814. At the Battle of Horseshoe Bend, while the whites fought on one side, the Cherokee managed to sneak across the river

Cherokee soldiers were full members of the U.S. Army during the war with the Red Stick Creek.

During the war with the Red Stick Creek, the Cherokee considered Andrew Jackson a friend. They called him the Pointed Arrow. But once the war was over, Jackson's dealings with the Cherokee took a dramatic turn. Immediately after the war, Jackson proposed that the military take over Cherokee and Chickasaw land in Tennessee. A few years later, he bullied the Cherokee into giving up two large areas of land in Georgia and Tennessee in the Treaty of 1817. Jackson became despised by the Cherokee, who changed his name to the Chicken Snake.

and attack the Red Sticks from the other side. Because of this brave action, the United States defeated the Red Sticks, bringing the war to an end. Sequoyah was discharged on April 11, 1814. He was paid $66.80 for 147 days of service.

With the war over, Sequoyah returned home to Tuskegee. By this time, Sequoyah had a family. Although there is no record of a marriage, Sequoyah had at least one child, a son named Teesee who was born around 1800.

Sequoyah's family expanded in 1815 when he married a woman named Sally Waters who was half Cherokee. She was from the Bird Clan, and at 26 years old, she was more than 10 years younger than her husband.

Although Sally is the only wife Sequoyah is known for certain to have had, some historians believe that he had at least one other wife, a Cherokee woman named U-ti-yu, whom he wed sometime after his marriage to Sally. It was not uncommon at that time for a Cherokee man to be married to more than one woman at a time, and Sequoyah may have been married to U-ti-yu while he was also married to Sally.

Outside of his home and family, Sequoyah took on a diplomatic role. In 1816, he was chosen as a delegate to represent his people during a meeting with the U.S. government—the first of many positions of civic importance he would hold. He and 15 other Cherokee men met with Andrew Jackson to discuss a disputed land treaty. Sequoyah used his English name, George Guess, to sign the new treaty, which ceded Cherokee claims to 3,500 square miles (9,100 square km) of land in Alabama and Georgia in return for $5,000 and an annuity of $6,000 for six years. This treaty did not directly affect Sequoyah personally, but another treaty three years later did.

The Treaty of 1819 was the 25th treaty between the Cherokee and the U.S. government. As in most of the treaties, the United States again promised that the tribal borders would be guaranteed and would not be crossed by white settlers. Once again, the Cherokee believed

Sequoyah was known as a Cherokee traditionalist. Although other Cherokee adopted the clothes of white men and spoke some English, Sequoyah rejected the white culture and was faithful to the old Cherokee ways. He wore traditional Cherokee clothes, including moccasins, leggings, a hunting jacket, and a turban. He also refused to speak, read, or write English, even though his wife and many of his friends were bilingual.

the United States and agreed to it. In this treaty, they gave up about 6,000 square miles (15,600 square km), approximately one-fourth of their total land.

Some of the land that was ceded was the area around Tuskegee, and Sequoyah and his family were forced to leave their home. By this time, Sequoyah's family had grown to include several children. Records show his family members numbered anywhere from five to 12, but son Teesee and daughter Ahyokah are the only children known by name.

In the 1800s, treaties forced many Native American tribes to leave land they had occupied for hundreds of years.

Sequoyah, Sally, and the rest of the family packed up their things and started the difficult move. They

had no wagon to haul their belongings, so they and their horses carried everything. Anything they could not carry had to be left behind. A table and five chairs, a plow and harness, a saddle, a spinning wheel, and their cattle were among the items they left. These items were probably claimed by the white family who took over their home shortly after their departure.

Sequoyah and his family traveled south and finally settled in Willstown, the area that is now Fort Payne, Alabama. There they started a new life for themselves, and Sequoyah began to work on the invention that would make him one of the most famous and respected Cherokee in history. ᎤᎾ

Cherokee Alphabet.

D *a*	R *e*	T *i*	Ꮼ *o*	O *u*	i *v*
S *ga* Ꝺ *ka*	Ᏺ *ge*	Ᏹ *gi*	A *go*	J *gu*	E *gv*
Ꮣ *ha*	Ᏸ *he*	Ꭿ *hi*	Ᏺ *ho*	Ꮁ *hu*	Ꮗ *hv*
W *la*	Ꮁ *le*	Ꮅ *li*	H *mi*	M *mn*	Ꮈ *lv*
Ꮭ *ma*	Ꮧ *me*	H *mi*	Ꮵ *mo*	Ᏸ *mu*	
Ꮎ *na* Ꮏ *hna* Ᏻ *nah*	Ꭺ *ne*	ᏝᏝ *ni*	Z *no*	Ꮖ *nu*	Ꮙ *nv*
Ꮖ *qua*	Ꮽ *que*	Ꮙ *qui*	V *quo*	Ꮗ *quu*	Ꮗ *quv*
Ꮜ *sa* Ꮝ *s*	4 *se*	Ꮁ *si*	Ꮩ *so*	Ꮯ *su*	R *sv*
Ꮜ *da* W *ta*	Ꮢ *de* Ꮟ *te*	Ꮧ *di* Ꭲ *ti*	V *do*	S *du*	Ꮣ *dv*
Ꮬ *dla* Ꮮ *lla*	L *tle*	C *tli*	Ꮴ *tlo*	Ꮲ *tlu*	P *tlv*
Ꮳ *tsa*	V *tse*	Ᏼ *tsi*	K *tso*	Ꮪ *tsu*	C *tsv*
Ꮐ *wa*	Ꮼ *we*	Ꮎ *wi*	Ꮼ *wo*	Ꮗ *wu*	6 *wv*
Ꮿ *ya*	B *ye*	Ꮽ *yi*	Ꮵ *yo*	G *yu*	B *yv*

Chapter
4 TAMING A WILD ANIMAL

⚬◦∽◦⚬

No one is sure what event first prompted Sequoyah to try to find a way to write the Cherokee language. Some people believe he was thinking about a writing system as early as 1809, but it seems that he did not work much on it until after his move to Willstown. His first attempts involved drawing a picture or image for each word. At first, he used a knife or a nail to make the marks on pieces of bark. He soon decided that this process was too tiring. He then got a quill pen, made ink from tree bark, and started to write on paper.

Thousands of pictures later, Sequoyah realized that there were simply too many words, and not even he could remember all of the pictures he had drawn. He gave up on pictures and next started to work with

In creating a writing system for the Cherokee language, Sequoyah borrowed symbols that he had seen in written English.

Some Cherokee believed that they should not learn to read and write. They believed an old tribal story in which the Creator gave the Cherokee and the white man each a gift. The Cherokee received a book and the white man a bow and arrows. But the Cherokee neglected the book, and the white man stole it and left the bow and arrows in its place. The Cherokee believed that because the first Cherokee had lost the right to the book, from then on, reading and writing belonged to the white people.

signs and symbols. At first, he tried to make a symbol that stood for a sentence, but that didn't work. Then he attempted to create a symbol for every word. But as with the pictures, there were simply too many to remember.

Throughout the years that Sequoyah worked on developing the written language, he was often criticized by his family, friends, and neighbors. Sequoyah became so obsessed with writing that he neglected everyone and everything else. He even built a small hut behind his family's house so he could work without interruption. His wife and children were left to fend for themselves, and the farm's fields became overrun with weeds and grass. Many people who met Sequoyah's family and saw his farm believed that Sequoyah was lazy and irresponsible for not taking better care of his family and property. Other people noticed the marks he was making on bark and paper and believed that he was practicing witchcraft or "bad magic." Most of his friends avoided him because they believed he was

foolish or crazy.

One day, Sequoyah's friend Turtle Fields visited him and said:

> *My friend, there are a great many remarks upon this employment you have taken up. Our people are most concerned about you. They think you are wasting your life. They think, my friend, that you are making a fool of yourself, and will no longer be respected.*

Sequoyah replied:

> *If our people think I am making a fool of myself, you may tell them that what I am doing will not make fools of them. They did not cause me to begin, and they shall not cause me to stop. If I am no longer respected, what I am doing will not make our people less respected, either by themselves or others; so I shall go on, and you may tell our people.*

Sequoyah wore the traditional Cherokee dress, including a turban.

Sequoyah's wife, Sally, eventually lost patience with him. The work that he was doing in his little hut was clearly not good for him or his family, she thought. One day while he was out of the hut, Sally and the neighbors burned down the hut and everything in it. But when Sequoyah returned and found his work reduced to ashes, he simply started again.

This time in Sequoyah's life must have been very frustrating for him. He endured many setbacks, and it seemed that everything he tried failed. But as Sequoyah later said, he believed that if he could figure out how to put sounds on paper, "it would be like catching a wild animal and taming it." And so he continued the chase.

Finally, Sequoyah had a breakthrough. He realized that a word could be broken down into parts, or syllables, that were sometimes repeated in other words. Sequoyah worked at separating each word until he had isolated all of the syllables in the Cherokee language. There were 86. He then made a symbol for each syllable. Some of the symbols he created himself; other symbols he borrowed from the English alphabet.

People differ about where Sequoyah saw the English letters. Some say he used a spelling book. Others say he found a piece of newspaper or a diary. His brother-in-law, Michael Waters, recalled:

> *Sequoyah was studying for characters to make use of in printing and ... he copied some of the letters from the Waters family Bible and said these would do for print.*

The Cherokee language, called Tsalagi, comes from the Iroquoian family of languages. The original 86 symbols of the written form were later reduced by one. The remaining 85 symbols represent six vowels, an "s" sound, and 78 symbols that stand for combinations of consonants and vowels. Tsalagi does not have the sounds that are represented in English by the letters B, F, J, P, R, V, X, and Th. However, the Cherokee language includes a vowel that does not exist in English.

A syllabary is one of three basic systems of writing. In a logographic system, each written character represents an individual word. Chinese is an example of this writing system. In an alphabetic system, of which English is an example, characters stand for vowels or consonants—the most basic sounds that make up a language. In a syllabic writing system, a set of characters represents the syllables of a language, the next largest unit of sound in a language. A syllable consists of a vowel sound or a consonant-vowel combination. Syllabaries typically contain many more characters than alphabets but much fewer than logographic systems.

Whatever the source, Sequoyah made these symbols his own by turning them or adding details to them.

Because Sequoyah's system was based on syllables, his invention was called a syllabary. This syllabary was the key to writing the Cherokee language. The symbols could be written down and grouped together to form words. For the first time, the Cherokee were able to write down the words that they had been speaking for centuries.

Over thousands of years, each Native American tribe in North America had developed its own spoken language, but until Sequoyah made his syllabary, no tribe had a complete written language. Only the whites in America had a way to write their language, and that system had developed over many centuries. Many white missionaries had attempted to write down the Native American languages, including the Cherokee language, but none of them had succeeded.

FACSIMILE OF CHEROKEE ALPHABET BEFORE PRINTING.

1 A, short. 2 A broad. 3 Lah. 4 Tsee. 5 Nah. 6 Weeh. 7 Weh. 8 Leeh. 9 Neh. 10 Mooh. 11 Keeh 12 Yeeh. 13 Seeh. 14 Clanh. 15 Ah. 16 Luh. 17 Leh. 18 Hah. 19 Woh. 20 Cloh. 21 Tah. 22 Yahn. 23 Lahn. 24 Hee. 25 Ss (sibilant.) 26 Yoh. Un (French.) 28 Hoo. 29 Goh. 30 Tsoo. 31 Maugh. 32 Seh. 33 Saugh. 34 Cleegh. 35 Queegh. 36 Quegh. 37 Sah. 38 Quah. 39 Gnaugh (nasal.) 40 Kaah. 41 Tsahn 42 Sahn. 43 Neeh. 44 Kah. 45 Taugh. 46 Keh. 47 Taah. 48 Khan. 49 Weeh. 50 Eeh. 51 Ooh. 52 Yeh. 53 Un. 54 Tun. 55 Kooh. 56 Tsoh. 57 Quoh. 58 Noo. 59 Na. 60 Loh. 61. Yu. 62 Tseh. 63 Tee. 64 Wahn. 65 Tooh. 66 Teh. 67 Tsah. 68 Un. 69 Neh. 70 —— 71 Tsooh. 72 Mah. 73 Clooh. 74 Haah. 75 Hah. 76 Meeh. 77 Clah. 78 Yah. 79 Wah. 80 Teeh. 81 Clegh. 82 Naa. 83 Quh. 84 Clah. 85 Maah 86 Quhn.

With the completion of his syllabary, Sequoyah had achieved what no single person had done before: He had created a written language. Moreover, what he had just done in a matter of years had taken centuries for the whites to accomplish. For his amazing accomplishment, Sequoyah would become known as a Cherokee genius. But first he had to make his syllabary known and accepted and teach people how to use it. Ꮙ

Although many of Sequoyah's symbols look like English letters, they do not sound like them.

Chapter

5 SPREADING LIKE FIRE

❧⟡❧

As soon as his syllabary was finished, Sequoyah began to use it for everything. With it, he could write whatever he wished. He made notes, kept records, and wrote accounts of his money. What a wonderful gift this would be for his people! But first he had to convince them that he wasn't crazy and that his syllabary did indeed work.

Telling people about the syllabary and convincing them of its usefulness was not as easy as it sounded. Most people refused to listen to Sequoyah when he tried to teach them. Perhaps they had heard too many negative stories about him. So Sequoyah traveled to Arkansas to tell the Cherokee there about the syllabary. They didn't believe him either and thought it was a trick. Sequoyah finally asked one man there to send a message to a friend in the East. Sequoyah would write down the message and give it to the friend. The man told Sequoyah a message, and Sequoyah wrote it down and left. When Sequoyah arrived in the East, he delivered the letter and read the message in front of many people. Some people were amazed and were convinced that Sequoyah could write and read Cherokee, but many believed he had simply memorized the message and repeated it, as the Cherokee had done for hundreds of years.

Sequoyah then invited the Cherokee Tribal Council to test his syllabary. Sequoyah waited outside while the chiefs gave a message to Ahyokah, Sequoyah's 6-year-old daughter. Ahyokah wrote it down, and when Sequoyah came into the room, he read the message. Still, some chiefs were not convinced. But they agreed to watch another demonstration.

Although Ahyokah was the first to demonstrate mastery of written Cherokee, she was not the first to learn the new syllabary. Sequoyah's brother-in-law, Michael Waters, was his first student, and Waters' son was his second.

This time, the Tribal Council made sure there was no possibility of deception. They brought in several bright, reliable young men and had Sequoyah teach them his syllabary. The council then separated the young men and told each one a different message. Each young man wrote down the message and handed the paper to the council. With all of the messages complete,

the papers were shuffled and handed out to the young men so each had a paper different from the one he had written. The council then asked the young men to read the messages in their hands. The young men did so, and the council was convinced—Sequoyah

Black Coat, a Cherokee chief painted in the 1800s by artist George Catlin, wore a feathered headdress and carried a pipe.

was indeed offering his people the gift of a written language. Soon after the demonstrations, the Cherokee Nation officially accepted the syllabary, and Cherokee people everywhere began to hear about Sequoyah's invention.

In 1824, a white missionary named William Chamberlin commented, "The knowledge of Mr. Guess's [syllabary] is spreading like fire among the brush." By that time—only three years after the Cherokee Nation had accepted Sequoyah's work—a majority of the Cherokee people could already read and write in their own language. Thousands had become literate in the first year alone. To the rest of the world, it seemed that the Cherokee had become a literate people overnight.

Learning the syllabary was nothing like going to school and learning to read and write in English. For one thing, the syllabary was much easier for a Cherokee to learn than English. A good student often had to go to school for several years before being able to read and write in English. But with the syllabary, many could learn to read and write in just a few days. And learning the syllabary did not require sitting in a stuffy schoolhouse or listening to a strict schoolteacher. The syllabary could be learned anywhere and anytime. Trees, boards, fences, walls of houses, and bits of bark served as blackboards for improvised "schools." Knives, pieces of coal, and paint served as chalk. And anyone could teach. Friends taught friends, strangers taught strangers, and the syllabary spread from village to village across the Cherokee Nation.

DᏢGWⴅ

ᎫᎾᏓᎣᎥᎯ ᎫᎾᏍᏕᏗᏬᎯ.

CHEROKEE PRIMER.

PARK HILL:
Mission Press. John Candy, Printer.
DᎾ ᎣᎯᏴᏴᏝᏒ: ᎠᏋᎽᎯᏋ, ᎫᏍᏴᏬᎣᎵ.
::::::::
1845.

An 1845 schoolbook was printed in Cherokee and English.

45

Having a way to write their language transformed and unified the Cherokee Nation. At last, the Cherokee in one area could communicate with friends and family who lived far away. More important, the Cherokee were finally able to write down and preserve important tribal knowledge. Before the syllabary, all knowledge was passed from generation to generation by word of mouth. People had to remember everything because there was no way to write anything down and no way to find the information anywhere else. With the syllabary, medicine men could write down their sacred formulas and rituals. They no longer had to worry about their work being changed or ruined because of a forgotten or added word. Political leaders no longer had to translate their documents into English. They could now make documents in their own language, and all Cherokee could finally know what was said in those documents. Thus the syllabary enabled the Cherokee to keep records and preserve their history.

The need to preserve their history and identity was becoming increasingly important to the Cherokee people. Throughout the 1820s, white settlers continued to push into Cherokee land. In the early 1820s, they pushed into the area around Willstown, where Sequoyah and his family lived. Like most of the peaceful Cherokee, Sequoyah decided to move rather than fight the whites. His son Teesee, now married and a farmer, decided to stay.

In 1824, Sequoyah and his family moved west. Once again, they had no wagon and had to walk most of the way. After many days of travel, they arrived in Arkansas and settled near present-day Scottsville, about 15 miles (24 km) north of the Arkansas River. Sequoyah chose that location because there was a salt spring nearby and the blue-green mountains reminded him of his home at Tuskegee.

Many of the Cherokee in Arkansas created successful lives for themselves. They thrived as farmers. They tended fields of corn and cotton and raised

By the mid-19th century, many Cherokee had adopted the dress of white Americans.

cattle, pigs, and poultry. They built sturdy, comfortable homes of brick or stone. A visitor to the area remarked that the Cherokee were better dressed than their white counterparts to the south.

At his new home on the banks of the Arkansas River in the Illinois Bayou, Sequoyah continued to work at blacksmithing, did some farming, and began to manufacture salt from the nearby salt spring. He also worked to spread the use of his syllabary. Sequoyah gave out copies of the syllabary and taught it to anyone who asked. He never charged for the syllabary and would not accept money for it. When some people asked Sequoyah about this practice, he said some people could not afford to pay, so he would not charge anyone. His work helped spread literacy throughout the Cherokee in Arkansas.

By this point, Sequoyah, whom many had once called crazy, had become respected and famous among his people. The Cherokee National Council honored him with a medal that was inscribed in Cherokee and English:

A syllabary would not work well for the English language. English syllables are made up of many different combinations of vowels and consonants, and there are thousands of different syllables. In order to write English using a syllabary, each of these thousands of syllables would need to have its own symbol. There are, however, a few English words and phrases that can be written using letters as syllables: MT (empty); EZ (easy); NME (enemy); ICU (I see you); RUOK? (Are you okay?).

Presented to George Gist, by the General Council of the Cherokee Nation, for his ingenuity in the Invention of the Cherokee Alphabet, 1825.

A note from Cherokee leader John Ross accompanied the medal. It read:

The old and the young find no difficulty in learning to read and write in their native language. Types have been made and a printing press established in the Nation. The Scriptures have been translated and printed in Cherokee. While posterity continues to be benefited by the discovery, your name will be held in grateful remembrance. The great good designed by the author of human existence in directing your genius to this happy discovery cannot be fully estimated—it is incalculable. Wishing you health and happiness, I am, your friend, John Ross.

Sequoyah did not immediately receive his medal because the Cherokee National Council wanted to wait until it could be presented to him in person. Sequoyah did not return to the East to receive it, however, so it was finally sent to him in 1832. He treasured the medal and wore it constantly. Historians believe the medal was with him when he died and that it was buried with him.

ᏣᎳᎩ PROTECTION ᏗᎧᎿᏫᏍᏗ

CHEROKEE PHŒNIX.

VOL. I.   NEW ECHOTA, THURSDAY FEBRUARY 21, 1828.   **NO. 1.**

EDITED BY ELIAS BOUDINOTT,
PRINTED WEEKLY BY
ISAAC H. HARRIS,
FOR THE CHEROKEE NATION.

At $2 50 if paid in advance, $3 in six months, or $3 50 if paid at the end of the year.

To subscribers who can read only the Cherokee language the price will be $2 00 in advance, or $2 50 to be paid within the year.

Every subscription will be considered as continued unless subscribers give notice to the contrary before the commencement of a new year.

The Phoenix will be printed on a Super Royal sheet, with type entirely new procured for the purpose. Any person procuring six subscribers, and becoming responsible for the payment, shall receive a seventh gratis.

Advertisements will be inserted at seventy-five cents per square for the first insertion, and thirty-seven and a half cents for each continuance; longer ones in proportion.

☞ All letters addressed to the Editor, post paid, will receive due attention.

A GOOD CONSCIENCE.

What is there, in all the pomp of the world, the enjoyments of luxury, or the gratification of passion, comparable to the tranquility of a good conscience? to the health of the mind. It is a sweet perfume, that diffuses its fragrance every every thing that is without exhausting its store. Unaccompanied with this, the gay pleasures of the world are like brilliants to a diseased eye, music to a deaf ear, wine to an ardent fever, or dainties to the languor of an ague. To lie down on the pillow, after a day spent in temperance in beneficence, and piety, how sweet is it! How different from the state of him, who reclines, at an unnatural hour, with his blood inflamed, his head throbbing with wine and gluttony, his heart aching with rancorous malice, his thoughts totally estranged from Him who has protected him in the day, and will watch over him, ungrateful as he is, in the night season! A good conscience is, indeed, the peace of God. Passions lulled to sleep, clear thoughts, cheerful temper, a disposition to be pleased with every obvious and innocent object around, if these are the effects of a good conscience if these are the things that constitute happiness; and these condescend to dwell with the poor man, in his humble cottage in the vale of obscurity. In the magnificent mansion of the proud and vain, glitter the exteriors of happiness, the gilding, the trapping, the pride and the pomp; but is the decent habitation of piety is oftener found the domestic rest of heavenly peace; that solid good, of which the parade of the vain, the frivolous and voluptuous, is but a shadowy semblance.

Christian Philos ophy.

Flattery.—Few things are more universally condemned than flattery; yet there are few men, who are above its influence, and still fewer, who have courage sufficient to repel it with a faithful rebuke. The following anecdote is recommended, as affording a specimen of a good answer to flatterers. A certain clergyman in New England, eminent both for talents and humility, was one day accosted by a parishioner, who commended some of his performances of which the clergyman himself had a very low opinion. After just hearing him a few moments, the clergyman replied; "My Friend, if I had known better than that you was going to be no better opinion of myself than I had before, that you had a worse opinion of you."

CONSTITUTION OF THE CHEROKEE NATION,

Formed by a Convention of Delegates from the several Districts, at New Echota, July 1827.

WE, THE REPRESENTATIVES of the people of the Cherokee Nation in Convention assembled, in order to establish justice, ensure tranquility, promote our common welfare, and secure to ourselves and our posterity the blessings of liberty; acknowledging with humility and gratitude the goodness of the sovereign Ruler of the Universe, in offering us an opportunity so favorable to the design, and imploring his aid and direction in its accomplishment, do ordain and establish this Constitution for the Government of the Cherokee Nation.

ARTICLE I.

Sec. 1. THE BOUNDARIES of this nation, embracing the lands solemnly guaranteed and reserved forever to the Cherokee Nation by the Treaties concluded with the United States, are as follows; and shall forever hereafter remain unalterably the same—to wit:—Beginning on the North Bank of Tennessee River at the upper part of the Chickasaw old fields; thence along the main channel of said river, including all the islands therein, to the mouth of the Hiwassee river, thence up the main channel of said river, including Islands, to the first hill which closes in on said river, about two miles above Hiwassee old Town; thence along the ridge which divides the waters of the Hiwassee and little Tellico, to the Tennessee river at Tallassee; thence along the main channel including islands, to the junction of the Cowee and Nantayalee; thence along the ridge in the fork of said river, to the top of the blue ridge; thence along the blue ridge to the Unicoy Turnpike road; thence by a straight line to the main source of the Chestatee; thence along its main channel, including Islands, to the Chattahoochy; and thence down the same to the Creek boundary at Buzzard Roost; thence along the boundary line which separates this and the Creek Nation, to a point on the Coosa river opposite the mouth of Wills Creek; thence down along the South bank of the same to a point opposite to Fort Strother; thence up the river to the mouth of Wills Creek; thence up along the East bank of said creek, to the West branch thereof, and up the same to its source; and thence along the ridge which separates the Tombecbee and Tennessee waters, to a point on the top of said ridge; thence due North to Camp Coffee on Tennessee river, which is opposite the Chickasaw Island; thence to the place of beginning.

Sec. 2. The Sovereignty and Jurisdiction of this Government shall extend over the Country within the boundaries above described, and the lands therein are, and shall remain, the common property of the Nation; but the improvements made thereon, and in the possession of the citizens respectively who made, or may rightfully be in possession of them; *Provided,* That the citizens of the Nation, possessing exclusive and indefeasible right to their respective improvements, as expressed in this article, shall possess no right nor power to dispose of their improvements in any manner whatever to the United States, individual States, nor to individual citizens thereof; and that, whenever any such citizen or citizens shall remove with their effects out of the limits of this Nation, and become citizens of any other Government, all their right and privileges as citizens of this Nation shall cease; *Provided nevertheless,* That the Legislature shall have power to re-admit by law to all the rights of citizenship, any such person or persons, who may at any time desire to return to the Nation on their memorializing the General Council for such

readmission. Moreover, the Legislature shall have power to adopt such laws and regulations, as its wisdom may deem expedient and proper, to prevent the citizens from monopolizing improvements with the view of speculation.

ARTICLE II.

Sec. 1. THE POWER of this Government shall be divided into three distinct departments;—the Legislative, the Executive, and the Judicial.

Sec. 2. No person or persons, belonging to one of these Departments, shall exercise any of the powers properly belonging to either of the others, except in the cases hereinafter expressly directed or permitted.

ARTICLE III.

Sec. 1. THE LEGISLATIVE POWER shall be vested in two distinct branches; a Committee, and a Council; each to have a negative on the other, and both to be styled, the General Council of the Cherokee Nation; and the style of their acts and laws shall be,

"RESOLVED by the Committee and Council in General Council convened."

Sec. 2. The Cherokee Nation, as laid off into eight Districts, shall so remain.

Sec. 3. The Committee shall consist of two members from each District, and the Council shall consist of three members from each District, to be chosen by the qualified electors of their respective Districts for two years; and the elections to be held in every District on the first Monday in August for the year 1828, and every succeeding two years thereafter; and the General Council shall be held once a year, to be convened on the second Monday of October in each year, at New Echota.

Sec. 4. No person shall be eligible to a seat in the General Council, but a free Cherokee Male citizen, who shall have attained to the age of twenty-five years. The descendants of Cherokee men by all free women, except the African race, whose parents may be or have been living together as man and wife, according to the customs and laws of this Nation, shall be entitled to all the rights and privileges of this Nation, as well as the posterity of Cherokee women by all free men. No person who is of negro or mulatto parentage, either by the father or mother side, shall be eligible to hold any office of profit, honor or trust, under this Government.

Sec. 5. The Electors, and members of the General Council, shall, in all cases except those of treason, felony, or breach of the peace, be privileged from arrest during their attendance at election, and at the General Council, and in going to and returning from, the same.

Sec. 6. In all elections by the people, the electors shall vote viva voce. Electors for members to the General Council for 1828, shall be held at the places of holding the several courts, and at the other two precincts in each District which are designated by the law under which the members of this Convention were elected; and the District Judges shall superintend the elections within the precincts of their respective Court Houses, and the Marshals & Sheriffs shall superintend within the precincts which may be assigned them by the Circuit Judges of their respective Districts, together with one other person, who shall be appointed by the Circuit Judges for each precinct within their respective Districts; and the Circuit Judges shall appoint a clerk to each precinct.—The superintendents and clerks shall, on the Wednesday morning succeeding the election, assemble at their respective Court Houses and proceed to examine and ascertain the true state of the polls, and shall issue to each member, duly elected, a certificate; and also make an official return of the state of the polls of election to the principal Chief, and it shall be the du-

[The remaining columns are printed in the Cherokee syllabary.]

6 THE PHOENIX RISES

ᙗᙒᙈ

Use of Sequoyah's syllabary was spreading rapidly, and demand was growing for materials to be printed in Cherokee. In 1825, tribal leaders decided to get a printing press that would print their language. White missionaries, hoping to spread their religion through the press, helped the Cherokee carry out the plan. Buying a printing press was the easy part. The hard part was getting the press to print the Cherokee language. Each of the symbols of the syllabary had to be made out of metal so it could be inserted into the printing press. The process was difficult for the men in Boston who had to form the metal shapes. The men were used to the 26 letters of the English alphabet, so the Cherokee symbols looked strange and too numerous.

The first edition of the Cherokee Phoenix *was published on February 21, 1828, and was printed in Cherokee and English.*

Getting a printing press ready to print was long, hard work. To make type, the letters or symbols used in a printing press, each letter or symbol had to be carved into a steel punch. The punch was then hammered into a piece of copper. The form made in the copper was put into a mold, and liquid metal was poured into it. When the metal hardened, it looked like the letter or symbol, only backward. The metal was then put on a small block of lead called a base.

To print a word, the printer selected the correct

The printing process of the 19th century was complicated and time-consuming.

type and lined it up in a frame. When all of the words for a page were ready, the printer put the full frame in the press. He put ink on the type and then used the printing press to push a sheet of paper onto the type. When the paper was lifted, the words were on the page. The printer could continue to ink the type and print as many copies as he wanted before changing the type for another page.

While the printing press and its symbols were being readied, the Cherokee built a print shop at the Cherokee Nation's capital in New Echota, Georgia. The building was a small, one-story log structure about 20 feet by 30 feet (6 meters by 9 meters). There was a door at each end and windows on the sides. The printing press, with its Cherokee type, was placed in the building in late January 1828.

On February 21, 1828, the first issue of the Cherokee newspaper was printed. In Cherokee, the newspaper's name was *Tsa'lagi' Tsu'llehisanun'hi,* which meant something like "I will rise." In English, the name was the *Cherokee Phoenix.* The word *phoenix* was a reference to a bird in an ancient Egyptian myth that rose from its own ashes. The phoenix was an

> *According to an Egyptian myth, the phoenix was a male bird with beautiful red and gold feathers. Every 500 years, the phoenix would make a nest and then set fire to it. Both the nest and the bird would burn entirely, and a new phoenix would arise from the ashes.*

Elias Boudinot
(1803–1839)

important symbol for the Cherokee, who believed that, like that bird, their culture would again rise to greatness.

First edited by the young Cherokee intellectual Elias Boudinot, the *Cherokee Phoenix* was published weekly. Each issue was four pages long and included information both in Cherokee and English. Translating from English to Cherokee was slow and difficult, so there was always more English in the newspaper than Cherokee. The Cherokee people often read the parts of the paper that were in their own language and then went to a friend or neighbor who knew English to hear about the rest. The *Cherokee Phoenix* made people familiar with events going on in the world and likewise told the world about what was happening in the Cherokee Nation.

The newspaper gave its readers information that was very important to them at the time. The *Cherokee Phoenix* included public documents and the laws of the Cherokee Nation. For the first time, the

Cherokee could read and review their nation's own rules and regulations. The paper also had articles that discussed Cherokee culture and educational development. For the majority of its readers, however, the most important information the newspaper contained had to do with the relationship between the Cherokee Nation and the U.S. government. During the 1820s and throughout the 1830s, many white settlers were encouraging the government to push all Native Americans west of the Mississippi River. Through the *Cherokee Phoenix*, the Cherokee people learned what the U.S. government was planning to do.

The tribe's printing press published more than just the *Cherokee Phoenix*, however. It also printed parts of the Bible, hymnbooks, religious pamphlets, schoolbooks, and other materials.

Sequoyah was undoubtedly pleased and proud to see how far his invention had brought his people, but he had a longstanding distrust of the missionar-

In 1829, the Cherokee Phoenix changed its name to the Cherokee Phoenix and Indian Advocate to reflect Cherokee response to the growing public debate over Indian removal and to reflect a shift in the paper's content and editorial stand. Editor Elias Boudinot's increasingly pro-removal stance was at odds with the position of Cherokee Chief John Ross and led to his ouster as editor in 1832. Publication of the newspaper continued two more years under editor Elijah Hicks before it was stopped in 1834. Plans to resume publication were ruined when Georgians stole the press and type in 1835.

ies who were behind the Cherokee people's printing press. John F. Wheeler, the white printer of the *Cherokee Phoenix*, recalled that Sequoyah once told some missionaries that if he had known that they would use his syllabary to try to convert the Cherokee to their religion, he would never have invented it. Sequoyah had long resisted white attempts at conversion, as his friend Houston Benge explained:

The Brainerd Mission near present-day Chattanooga, Tennessee, included a school for Cherokee children as well as a church.

> *Sequoyah had but little faith in the white man, and could never be induced to embrace his religion, although the missionaries labored long and earnestly with him. ... He saw so many bad white men everywhere ... who were tolerated by society, that he had come to the conclusion that the white man's religion could not*

be a good one, or there would not be so many bad white people, who had cheated and robbed the Indians from the days they first landed on the shores of America. He thought that the missionaries instead of going out to convert the Indians, should try to convert the bad white people at home, who are worse than any Indians he had ever seen.

Contrary to Sequoyah's fears, the syllabary served not to convert the Cherokee but to elevate and unite them. Of the many ways the syllabary helped his people, the most important was the way it affected the Cherokee people's feelings about themselves. The syllabary gave a boost to the culture and unified the Cherokee Nation. Being able to read and write in their own language made Cherokee people everywhere very proud of themselves and their culture. The syllabary and the literacy that resulted from it showed that the Cherokee were intelligent people and were not inferior to whites. But the syllabary and its effects could not stop the white people's desire for more land and their plans to obtain it.

> *The syllabary was such a great gift for the Cherokee that Sequoyah wanted to give the same gift to other Native Americans. Using his syllabary as an example, he was able to make a syllabary for the Choctaw language. He hoped that all tribes would be able to adapt his syllabary and write in their own language.*

7 TREATIES AND TRAVELS

❧⥁⥀❧

In 1827, Sequoyah traveled to Washington, D.C., as a delegate for his people. The Cherokee were concerned about their land boundaries, which the U.S. government had said were guaranteed. But if the boundaries were guaranteed, they wondered, why didn't the government stop the white settlers from moving into Cherokee territory?

Sequoyah and the other delegates arrived in the U.S. capital in December and soon discovered that the government expected them to sign another treaty. This time, the government wanted to relocate all of the Cherokee who had settled along the Arkansas River. The delegates did their best to refuse, but the government officials would not take no for an answer. The delegates were reminded that

A copy of painter Charles Bird King's portrait of Sequoyah depicts the great Cherokee with his syllabary.

they had no way to return home unless the government arranged it. Government officials also bribed the delegates with money and other gifts. Still, the Cherokee delegates continued to refuse to sign the treaty.

Sequoyah's invention had brought him fame in the white community as well, and while he waited in Washington, he gave interviews to local journalists. Samuel Lorenzo Knapp recalled:

No stoic could have been more grave in his demeanor than was See-quah-yah; he pondered, according to the Indian custom, for a considerable time after each question was put, before he made his reply, and often took a whiff of his calumet while reflecting on an answer.

Charles Bird King painted portraits of more than 100 Native American leaders from more than 20 different tribes. This collection was placed in the Smithsonian Institution in Washington, D.C., in 1858. Nearly all of the paintings, including the portrait of Sequoyah, were destroyed when the central building of the Smithsonian burned in 1865.

He also sat for a portrait by artist Charles Bird King. This portrait was the only one ever painted of Sequoyah. It shows him as journalist Jeremiah Evarts described him at the time: about 50 years old and wearing typical Cherokee clothing—turban, cloak, leggings, and moccasins.

In May 1828, after six months of being essentially held captive, the tired and homesick Cherokee delegates agreed to sign the treaty. On the day of the signing, each of the delegates was given a new suit of clothes. Sequoyah, however, refused his and continued to wear his Cherokee clothing. When they signed the treaty, Sequoyah and three other delegates signed by using the syllabary symbols that made up their names.

The Treaty of 1828 changed the life of Sequoyah and approximately 600 other Cherokee families who lived along the Arkansas River. They had to give up their homes, fields, gardens, and orchards and move into the western wilderness, where they would have to start over again.

The interior of Sequoyah's home has been re-created at the Sequoyah Memorial in Sallisaw, Oklahoma.

Sequoyah and the others left Arkansas in 1829 and made the long, difficult journey to what is now Oklahoma. Once again, few of them had wagons, so they could take along only what they and their horses could carry. Many people had to leave without their cows, pigs, and chickens. Sequoyah and his family had to leave behind many things, including a whip saw, 10 large black kettles, and numerous ducks and chickens. Some Cherokee, including Sequoyah's wife, Sally, tried to sell some of their belongings before they left. But the white settlers nearby would not buy anything. They knew they could have everything for free once the Cherokee left.

Sequoyah and his family settled along the Arkansas River in the Skin Bayou, 11 miles (17.6 km) east of present-day Sallisaw, Oklahoma. Sequoyah worked hard and within a few years had built a comfortable home for his family. The farm had 10 acres (4 hectares) of fields, three small cabins, and several mules, oxen, cattle, and hogs. John Stuart, a U.S. military officer stationed in the area around this time, became acquainted with Sequoyah and offered this description:

> *George Guess ... is of a middle stature, and of rather a slender form. His features are remarkably regular and his face well formed, and rather handsome. His manner is agreeable, and his deportment gen-*

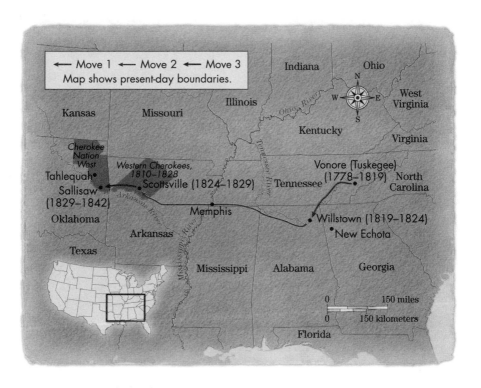

tlemanly. He poses a mild disposition, and is patient, but is energetic and extremely persevering and determined in the pursuit or accomplishment of any object on which he may fix his mind. He is inquisitive, and appears to be exceedingly desirous of acquiring information on all subjects. His mind seems to soar high and wide; and if he could have had the advantages of an enlightened education, he would have no doubt brought himself to rank high among the acknowledged great men of the age in which he lives.

Although Sequoyah continued to work as a

Sequoyah's many moves west were not unusual for Cherokee of the time.

Visitors can tour Sequoyah's cabin at the Sequoyah Memorial in Sallisaw, Oklahoma.

farmer and blacksmith, he now found employment as a teacher as well. Some people sent their children to him to learn to read and write in Cherokee. He was also known to ride to small towns in the area and teach the syllabary to anyone willing to learn.

In 1832, the Cherokee National Council hired Sequoyah to teach school in the Cherokee language. Sequoyah, who resented the missionaries' attempts to replace Cherokee traditions and values with those of white people, was pleased to teach in Cherokee, using the syllabary he had created.

It wasn't long before written Cherokee was being

used in the mission schools as well. The missionaries who ran these schools, however, disliked having Cherokee children learn in their native tongue. As one missionary explained:

> *Language stands closely identified with habits and prejudices, cherishes them and keeps them alive. These must be removed before any permanent change can be wrought in their condition and character.*

There are reports from Sequoyah's time that he may have kept a journal or been writing a history of the Cherokee people, but no such documents have ever been found.

But with the written language now used in the missionary schools, Cherokee literacy spread among the Western Cherokee, and tribal identity stayed strong.

8 UNITING THE NATION

ɔ⌒ɔ

Back in the East, the Cherokee who still lived in portions of Tennessee, Kentucky, Georgia, Alabama, and the Carolinas were losing their homeland. In 1828, the state of Georgia claimed that it owned all of the tribal land within its borders, and the United States government, under newly elected President Andrew Jackson, did nothing to stop the Georgians from violently forcing the Cherokee out of their homes.

By that time, some members of the federal government were working on a new way to solve the problems between the Cherokee and the white settlers. Their solution involved the relocation of all the Cherokee and other Eastern Native American tribes to an area west of the Mississippi River. President Jackson, once considered a friend to the Chero-

More than 4,000 Cherokee died on the forced journey west known as the Trail of Tears.

kee, supported and advocated this plan.

On May 28, 1830, President Jackson signed into law the Indian Removal Act. This law authorized the president to negotiate land-exchange treaties with tribes living within the boundaries of existing U.S. states. Native Americans were persuaded to give up their tribal lands in the East in exchange for monetary sums and land in Indian Territory, part of the vast land west of the Mississippi River that the United States had acquired in the Louisiana Purchase of 1803. Although some tribes negotiated and resettled in the West, the Cherokee struggled to maintain a grasp on their homeland.

In 1832, the Supreme Court ruled that the Cherokee Nation was its own community and had its own territory. Therefore, the people of Georgia had no right to enter that territory without permission from the Cherokee people. But the Georgians ignored the ruling, and President Jackson refused to enforce the court's decision.

While most Cherokee continued to trust that their legal rights would prevail and that they would be able to stay in their homeland, a small group of Cherokee believed that relocation was inevitable. The members of this group believed that the tribe should work with the U.S. government to arrange the best and safest conditions for relocation. The group was led by Major Ridge, his son John, and Elias

Boudinot, the former editor of the *Cherokee Phoenix.* They worked in opposition to Chief John Ross and the majority of the tribe, dividing the Cherokee Nation into the Ridge supporters and the Ross supporters.

On December 29, 1835, the Ridge party signed a treaty with the U.S. government at New Echota, Georgia. Although the group did not have the support of the tribe or the right to sign the treaty, the U.S. government said the treaty was legal. The Treaty of 1835, also called the Treaty of New Echota, sold all Cherokee land east of the Mississippi River to the United States for $5 million. All Cherokee living there had to leave the land and move west.

Major Ridge (1771–1839)

After many threats, approximately 5,000 Cherokee finally agreed to move. The rest clung to their homeland. In 1837, the U.S. government sent the Army to make sure that all of the Cherokee were evacuated. Over the next year, soldiers invaded Cherokee homes and marched families at bayonet point to stockades where they were held for months awaiting transportation to the West. Confined in cramped and dirty conditions, disease flourished, and many Cherokee died before their journey even began.

Major General Winfield Scott was in charge of gathering the Cherokee for their removal. He later wrote about the task in his autobiography:

> *Before the first night thousands—men, women, and children, sick and well— were brought in. Poor creatures. ... Many arrived half starved, but refused the food that was pressed upon them. At length, the children, with less pride, gave way, and next their parents. ... [I have] never witnessed a scene of deeper pathos [misery].*

Because many Cherokee were forced to leave with only the clothes on their backs, they were not prepared for the snow and cold of a winter journey.

The Cherokee traveled west in a series of migrations. Some Cherokee traveled by flatboat, going

down the Tennessee, Ohio, and Mississippi rivers and up the Arkansas River. Many more traveled over land in a 1,000-mile (1,600-km) march. Thousands died of starvation and disease, and summer drought and winter snows added to the mounting death toll. About one-fourth of the people died along the way, and the journey became known as the *Nunna daul Tsunyi*, or the Trail of Tears. For those who survived

The Trail of Tears covered 1,000 miles (1,600 km) and several states.

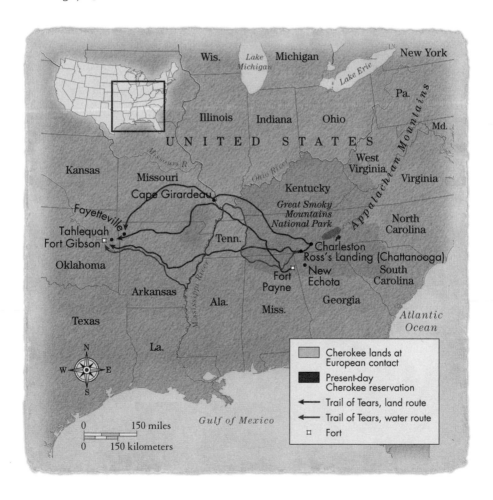

the journey, more problems awaited them in their new homeland.

In the Indian Territory west of the Mississippi River, the Eastern, or "Old Nation," Cherokee joined the Western Cherokee. But the people soon discovered that uniting these two parts of the Cherokee Nation would not be easy. Each had its own government. The Westerners believed the newcomers should live under the Western government, which was already well-established. The more numerous Easterners believed they should form a new government. Unification was further complicated by the continued division of the Eastern Cherokee between the Ridge supporters, now called the Treaty Party, and the Ross supporters, or the Ross Party. The struggle for control of the Cherokee government was complicated indeed.

Cherokee Chief John Ross (1790–1866)

Sequoyah became a mediator between the groups. He felt very strongly about the need for the Cherokee to live in unity and harmony. He believed that if they were divided, they would never reach greatness as a people. Sequoyah asked the Eastern and Western Cherokee to meet together in July 1839 to resolve their differences.

On July 1, about 2,000 Cherokee Indians gathered in Illinois with the hope of uniting the Cherokee Nation. Sequoyah served as one of two presidents of the conference. When the majority of the Western chiefs did not arrive, Sequoyah and the other president wrote a message to them. It read:

> *Shortly after their arrival in the West, the three leaders of the Treaty Party were murdered by followers of John Ross. Although Ross himself was never directly connected to the crimes and no one was ever charged, many of the victims' friends and followers believed the chief to have been involved, and their suspicions continued to divide the Cherokee Nation for many years.*

> *Friends and Brothers: In behalf of ourselves and the people of the eastern and western Cherokees, now in national convention at this place, we affectionately and respectfully invite you, together with the balance of our brethren, to repair to this place without delay, for the purpose of cooperating with us in promoting the peace, tranquility, and future prosperity and happiness of our common country.*

When the chiefs still did not come, Sequoyah sent another message:

The Cherokee were not the only Native Americans in the region called Indian Territory. They were grouped together with many tribes, including the Creek, Seminole, Chickasaw, and Choctaw, all of whom had been neighbors of the Cherokee in the Southeast. Groups of Plains Indians also lived in the area. The southeastern tribes were afraid of the Plains Indians, who still held to a hunter-warrior style of life.

We, the old settlers, are here in council with the late emigrants, and we want you to come up without delay, that we may talk matters over like friends and brothers. These people are here in great multitudes, and they are perfectly friendly towards us. They have said, over and over again, that they will be glad to see you, and we have full confidence that they will receive you with all friendship. ... We send you these few lines as friends, and we want you to come without delay, and bring as many of the old settlers as are with you; and we have no doubt but we can have all things amicably and satisfactorily settled.

One chief came, and the conference began. Over the next 11 days, Sequoyah gained the respect of both groups of Cherokee for his efforts to foster compromise and heal the divisions within the tribe.

On July 12, 1839, the Eastern and Western Cherokee were united with the signing of the Act of Union. Over the next few months, they wrote a constitution, organized a government, and established a capital at Tahlequah. Slowly, the Cherokee

The Cherokee Constitution was printed in the Cherokee language.

Nation began to rebuild itself in its new home, and Sequoyah started to think about ways to further unite his people. ❧

9 A Final Mission

Sequoyah had heard talk about a group of Cherokee who had moved south into Mexico years earlier. Sequoyah wanted all of his people to live together, so he began to plan a visit to Mexico. He would talk to these Cherokee and ask them to come back with him and live with the rest of the Cherokee Nation in Indian Territory.

In the spring of 1842, Sequoyah asked several men to go with him. One of the men was his son Teesee. Another was a friend known as the Worm. Sequoyah told the men that he wanted to visit the Western prairie and the Native Americans there. He did not tell them he planned to go all the way to Mexico. Teesee, the Worm, and six other men agreed to accompany Sequoyah. They did not ask questions about exactly

Artist Charles Banks Wilson's painting depicts Sequoyah at the beginning of his journey to Mexico to unite the Cherokee.

Sequoyah began his journey to Mexico in the grasslands of northeastern Oklahoma.

where they were going or why. They had great respect for Sequoyah and trusted his decisions and plans.

From the beginning, the journey was difficult for Sequoyah. The great Cherokee was now more than 60 years old and in poor health. Early in the trip, he began to suffer from severe chest pain and could not eat anything. His fellow travelers were not sure what to do. The Worm traveled to a Wichita village and bought some bread and hominy, a kind of treated corn. Sequoyah was able to eat this food and soon felt better. After another day's rest, the travelers continued on their way. Three days later, Sequoyah was feeling very ill again, and the group stopped again, this time at a Kichai village near the Red River. While there, Sequoyah sent home six of his followers. He asked only Teesee and the Worm to stay with him. His health improved a little, but he still had chest pains and had developed a bad cough.

Despite his poor health, Sequoyah was determined to continue on the journey. After leaving the Kichai village, Sequoyah finally told Teesee and the Worm that he planned to go to Mexico. He told them, "If I die, you can do what seems best to you. But while I'm alive be guided by me." Teesee and the Worm respected his wishes, and the three continued.

A short time later, the travelers came upon a group of Tawakoni Indians in central Texas who stole their horses and left them alone in

> *The Tawakoni Indians were one tribe in a group of Native Americans known as the Wichita Confederacy. The tribe probably started out in the area that is now Kansas, but by the 18th century, other tribes had pushed the Tawakoni south into present-day Texas. The theft of Sequoyah's horses was probably the Tawakonis' revenge for a Cherokee-led attack on a Tawakoni village in 1830.*

the wilderness. Teesee and the Worm were strong enough to travel on foot, but Sequoyah was much too weak. They needed to find a horse for him. While Sequoyah waited, Teesee and the Worm walked to a nearby village. But they soon returned to Sequoyah empty-handed. No one in the village would sell a horse to them.

Sequoyah believed there was only one solution to their problem. He told his son and his friend that they

Traditional Cherokee village life changed in the 19th century as more Native Americans turned to farming.

had to go to Mexico without him. There they would find the group of Cherokee and ask them for help. Surely their own people would give them horses. Then they could come back and get Sequoyah.

Teesee and the Worm may not have liked the idea of leaving Sequoyah by himself, but they agreed to his plan. Before they left, they found a cave south of the Colorado River and took Sequoyah to it. The cave would give Sequoyah shelter and a place to hide if more unfriendly people came. The river near the cave would provide him with fresh water. Teesee and the Worm also gave Sequoyah enough honey and venison to last him 20 days. Then Sequoyah's son and friend said goodbye and started on their walk to Mexico.

Sequoyah's stay in the cave began comfortably. He had food, water, and shelter. He also had a notebook in which to write, using the symbols he invented. But everything changed on the 12th day. A storm brought heavy rain, and water rushed into the cave. As the cave flooded, Sequoyah

The venison that Teesee and the Worm left for Sequoyah was probably dried venison. Native Americans often dried the meat of deer, buffalo, and other animals because there was no other way to preserve it. The meat was cut into thin strips and hung over a smoky fire until it was dry. Dried meat was good for journeys because it did not take up much room and satisfied hunger. Sometimes Native Americans pounded dried meat into a powder and mixed it with berries, bone marrow, and bear grease to make pemmican, another good traveling food.

grabbed two blankets and fled. He spent the night beneath a tree, huddled in the blankets and shivering from being cold and wet.

In the morning, Sequoyah built a fire. The small blaze warmed his body and dried his clothes and blankets. Feeling better, he went back to the cave to see if he could get his other belongings. When he looked inside, he saw that the cave was still filled with water. He had to wait.

A few days later, Sequoyah checked the cave again. The water was gone, but so was everything in it. The water had carried all of Sequoyah's things into the river, where they were rushed downstream. Sequoyah walked along the river for a while and eventually found his saddlebags, a tent, a brass kettle, and three more blankets. Everything else was lost.

Sequoyah was not sure what to do. He had no food, but he didn't want to leave the area near the cave, since Teesee and the Worm would expect him to be there when they returned. And so Sequoyah waited. Nearby, he found two trees where bees were making honey. Using only his tomahawk, Sequoyah slowly chopped at the trees until they fell. For the next few weeks, he ate honey and chewed on his deerskin shirt.

Sequoyah kept track of the days by making notches in a tree. After 40 days, the old Cherokee was convinced that something bad had happened to his son and friend. They were not coming back for him. He decided that he would try to reach Mexico on his own. Just in case someone came looking for him, he wrote a note and tied it to a tree branch by the cave.

Traveling was very difficult for Sequoyah. His crippled leg made walking very slow and painful. He was weak from lack of food. But he believed in what

Sequoyah traveled the entire length of Texas in his journey to unite the Cherokee people.

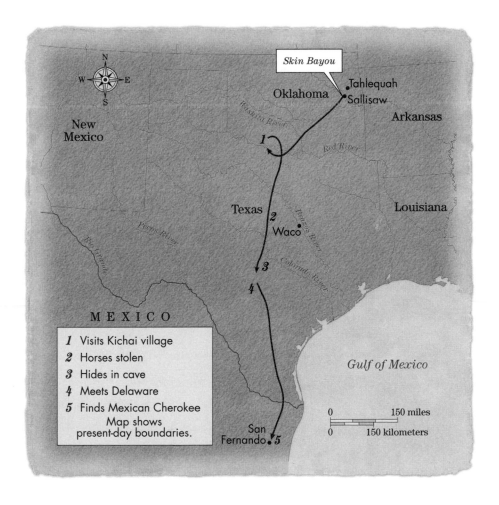

Skin Bayou

Tahlequah
Oklahoma   Sallisaw
                                    Arkansas

New
Mexico
1

Red River

Texas *2*
              Waco
                    3
              4
                                    Louisiana

M E X I C O

1 Visits Kichai village
2 Horses stolen
3 Hides in cave
4 Meets Delaware
5 Finds Mexican Cherokee
     Map shows
     present-day boundaries.

Gulf of Mexico

San
Fernando *5*

0   150 miles

0   150 kilometers

he was doing and found the strength to continue. He was not discouraged even when his path was blocked by a river. He built a raft and then used it to cross the river.

The Delaware Indians were a group of Native Americans who had once lived along the Delaware River. The Delaware were one of the first groups to come into contact with Europeans when the new settlers arrived in the early 1600s. Through a series of treaties with the U.S. government, the Delaware were moved farther and farther west, first to Ohio, then to Indiana, then to Missouri, then to Kansas, and finally to Indian Territory in present-day Oklahoma.

Farther south, Sequoyah met three friendly Native Americans riding on horses. They said they were from the Delaware tribe. The Delaware camped with Sequoyah for a few days and gave him fresh meat. They offered to take him home, but Sequoyah refused. Instead, he asked them to join him on his journey to Mexico. The three Delaware told him they could not go with him, but they would help him on his way. They gave him more meat and one of their horses. Sequoyah could now travel much more easily.

One evening, while Sequoyah was sitting by a fire, he heard several men on horses approaching. Were they friendly like the Delaware? Or would they take his horse like the Tawakoni had done? Sequoyah knew he would not be able to fight off any enemies, so he just waited quietly.

When the riders reached Sequoyah's camp, the

old Cherokee recognized two of the men—Teesee and the Worm. They were alive, and they had found him. Sequoyah was overjoyed.

Teesee and the Worm told Sequoyah about their journey. They had reached Mexico about 20 days after they left Sequoyah at the cave. Some Mexicans helped them reach a town where they met a man named Chief Standing Rock, the leader of the Cherokee who had settled in Mexico. Teesee and the Worm had told Standing Rock about Sequoyah and how he wanted to meet these Cherokee. The chief then helped Teesee and the Worm get horses and sent some of his group with them to get Sequoyah. Seventeen days later, the men had reached the cave and found it empty. But then they read Sequoyah's note and turned south again. They found Sequoyah's tracks and followed them until dark. Then they noticed a small fire in the distance and rode to see who was there. Now they were all sitting around that fire, thankful to have found Sequoyah at last.

The Mexican Cherokee took Sequoyah, Teesee, and the Worm back to their village near San Fernando. The Cherokee there welcomed them warmly. They were especially honored to have the famous Sequoyah with them.

Sequoyah felt he had almost achieved his goal. He had reached Mexico and had found the Cherokee there. Now he just had to bring these people back to the rest of the Cherokee Nation. Then all of his people would be united. But Sequoyah was not able to fulfill this last dream. His health worsened, and he

died in August 1843. He was buried in an unmarked grave near the Cherokee village in Mexico. Although the Cherokee there witnessed and mourned the great man's death, nearly two more years passed before the Cherokee Nation and the rest of the world learned of Sequoyah's fate. ☙

Missionaries at a San Fernando mission lived and worked among the Mexican Cherokee.

10 THE WORLD REMEMBERS A GENIUS

❧❀❧

By 1844, the people of the Cherokee Nation had real-ized that one of their most prominent citizens was missing. They knew only that Sequoyah had left his home and had gone into the southwestern wilder-ness. In February 1845, a $200 reward was offered to anyone willing to find Sequoyah and bring him home. Jesse Chisholm, a Cherokee-Scot frontiersman and possibly a relative of Sequoyah's, agreed to search for him.

In late June, a letter arrived at the Cherokee Nation. Signed by Chisholm and Chief Standing Rock, it reported the sad news that Sequoyah had died in August 1843.

When Chisholm returned to the Cherokee Nation, he completed Sequoyah's dream by bringing the Mex-

A statue of Sequoyah stands outside the Sequoyah Memorial in Sallisaw, Oklahoma.

A letter sent in 1845 informs an Indian reservation agent of Sequoyah's death and burial in Mexico.

ican Cherokee north. The group settled for a while on the Brazos River, near present-day Waco, Texas. Later, they moved farther north to the lower Washita River in present-day Oklahoma.

Although Sequoyah was gone, the world did not forget the Cherokee genius, his syllabary, or what he had done to unite the Cherokee. People around the world found ways to honor his memory. In 1847, Austrian botanist Stephen Endlicher named the great redwood trees on the West Coast of the United States. He called them *Sequoia sempervirens*, which means "ever-living Sequoyah." Later, when another group of amazing trees was discovered, the giant trees were named *Sequoiadendron giganteum*. Most people know them as the giant sequoia trees. In 1890, the U.S. Congress established a 386,560-acre (154,624-hectare) park in California and named it Sequoia National Park.

> *Sequoyah received the first lifetime pension ever granted by a Native American tribe. In 1841, the Cherokee Nation awarded him the pension in recognition of his syllabary. In December 1844, the Cherokee National Council replaced the first pension with a new pension of $300 per year. Since no one knew where Sequoyah was at the time, the pension was paid to his wife, Sally.*

The Cherokee Nation also made sure that Sequoyah was remembered. In 1851, the Nation changed the name of the area in which Sequoyah had lived. The name Skin Bayou District was changed to Sequoyah District.

In 1905, other tribes of Native Americans joined the Cherokee in another way to honor Sequoyah. The land known as Indian Territory was going to become

The giant sequoia trees of the West Coast are named in honor of the great Cherokee Sequoyah.

a state, and these people wanted the state to be called the State of Sequoyah. They even designed a state seal, which included an image of Sequoyah and his syllabary. But the U.S. Congress disagreed with the idea and, in 1907, named the state Oklahoma.

The people of Oklahoma later honored Sequoyah in other ways. In the early 1900s, they sent a statue of Sequoyah to Washington, D.C., to represent their state in Statuary Hall. In 1936, the Oklahoma Historical Society bought Sequoyah's farm near Sallisaw. The people in the society restored the cabin that Sequoyah had built and then had a large stone building put up over and around it. The building, called the Sequoyah Memorial of Oklahoma, is a National Historic Landmark. People can visit the building, see Sequoyah's cabin, and learn more about the time in which Sequoyah lived.

Many other places found different ways to honor Sequoyah. Georgia has a statue of him. A museum near Vonore, Tennessee, shows details about Sequoyah's life and Cherokee heritage. Many other places and things have been named after him, including a president's yacht, a nuclear power plant, numerous businesses, and a mountain on the Tennessee-North

A National Historic Landmark is a building, structure, object, or place that has an important significance in the history of the United States. National Historic Landmarks are often homes or workplaces of notable Americans; sites where important events took place; archeological sites that provide historically significant information; or places that characterize a particular culture or civilization. There are currently fewer than 2,500 National Historic Landmarks.

A statue of Sequoyah represents the state of Oklahoma in Statuary Hall.

Carolina border. All of these honors help to remind people about the great Cherokee.

Before the 1800s, no one would have guessed

that a genius would be found among the Chero-kee. Most white people believed that the Chero-kee and all Native Americans were savages. Per-haps even the Cherokee would have doubted that one of their people would become known as a genius. And yet Sequoyah became known and respected throughout the world as a man who achieved what no one had ever done before: He had single-handedly, and within a matter of years, created a written language. Sequoyah proved that people of any race or background can accomplish great things. ॐ

SEQUOYAH'S LIFE

1778

Born in Tuskegee, near present-day Vonore, Tennessee

1785

The U.S. government signs its first treaty with a Native American tribe, the Cherokee

1809

Starts to think about how to make a written language for the Cherokee

1800

1783

The Treaty of Paris ends the American Revolution

1809

Louis Braille of France, inventor of a writing system for the blind, is born

WORLD EVENTS

1813–1814

Joins Andrew
Jackson's forces
to fight the Red
Stick Creek

1815

Marries Sally Waters

1816

Signs his English
name, George Guess,
on a treaty with the
U.S. government

1815

1812–1814

The United States and
Britain fight the War
of 1812

1815

European states meet
in Vienna, Austria,
to redraw national
borders after the
conclusion of the
Napoleonic Wars

SEQUOYAH'S LIFE

1819

Is forced from his home in Tuskegee by the Treaty of 1819; moves to Willstown (present-day Fort Payne, Alabama)

1821

Demonstrates his syllabary to the Tribal Council; the Cherokee Nation accepts it

1824

Moves to Arkansas; settles near present-day Scottsville

1820

1821

Simon Bolivar frees Venezuela from Spanish rule

WORLD EVENTS

1825

Awarded medal by the Cherokee National Council for invention of the Cherokee syllabary

1827–1828

Serves as a delegate in Washington, D.C.; signs his name on the Treaty of 1828 using the symbols he created

1828

Using his syllabary, the first Native American newspaper, the *Cherokee Phoenix*, begins publication on February 21

1826

The first photograph is taken by Joseph Niépce, a French physicist

1828

Noah Webster publishes his dictionary, which contained more than 12,000 words that had never before appeared in a published dictionary

SEQUOYAH'S LIFE

1829

Moves west, settling near present-day Sallisaw, Oklahoma

1832

Hired by the Cherokee National Council to teach the Cherokee language in a Cherokee school

1838

U.S. government forces the Cherokee to move to Indian Territory (Oklahoma); many die on the Trail of Tears

1830

1829

The first practical sewing machine is invented by French tailor Barthélemy Thimonnier

1833

Great Britain abolishes slavery

1836

Texans defeat Mexican troops at San Jacinto after a deadly battle at the Alamo, giving Texas its independence

WORLD EVENTS

1839

Serves as a mediator
and helps unite the
Eastern and Western
Cherokee; they write
a new constitution

1842–1843

Journeys to Mexico
to find a "lost tribe"
of Cherokee

1843

Dies in August
near San Fernando,
Mexico

1840

1839

Scotsman Kirkpatrick
Macmillan completes
the first workable
bicycle; he calls it the
velocipede

1840

Auguste Rodin,
famous sculptor of
The Thinker is born

1844

Samuel Morse
perfects the
telegraph

DATE OF BIRTH: About 1778

BIRTHPLACE: Tuskegee, near present-day Vonore, Tennessee

FATHER: Nathaniel Gist (?–?)

MOTHER: Wurteh (?–1800?)

EDUCATION: No formal education

SPOUSE: Sally Waters (1789–?)

DATE OF MARRIAGE: 1815

CHILDREN: Sequoyah had several children, but the names of only a few are known:

Teesee (1800?–1867)

Ahyokah (1815?–?)

Unverified:
George Junior (?–1839)

Nancy (?–?)

Lightning Bug (?–?)

Wagon Wheel (?–?)

DATE OF DEATH: August 1843

PLACE OF BURIAL: Unmarked, undiscovered grave, probably near San Fernando, Mexico

FURTHER READING

Elish, Dan. *The Trail of Tears: The Story of the Cherokee Removal.* New York: Benchmark Books/Marshall Cavendish, 2002.

Klausner, Janet. *Sequoyah's Gift: A Portrait of the Cherokee Leader.* New York: HarperCollins, 1993.

Stewart, Mark. *The Indian Removal Act: Forced Relocation.* Minneapolis: Compass Point Books, 2007.

Stewart, Philip. *Cherokee.* Philadelphia: Mason Crest Publishers, 2004.

LOOK FOR MORE SIGNATURE LIVES BOOKS ABOUT THIS ERA:

James Beckwourth: *Mountaineer, Scout, and Pioneer*

Jim Bridger: *Trapper, Trader, and Guide*

Crazy Horse: *Sioux Warrior*

Geronimo: *Apache Warrior*

Sam Houston: *Texas Hero*

Jesse James: *Legendary Rebel and Outlaw*

Bridget "Biddy" Mason: *From Slave to Businesswoman*

Zebulon Pike: *Explorer and Soldier*

Sarah Winnemucca: *Scout, Activist, and Teacher*

On the Web

For more information on this topic,
use FactHound.

1. Go to *www.facthound.com*
2. Type in this book ID: 0756518873
3. Click on the *Fetch It* button.

FactHound will find the best Web sites
for you.

Historic Sites

The Sequoyah Birthplace Museum
576 Highway 360
P.O. Box 69
Vonore, TN 37885
423/884-6246
Exhibits showing the history and culture
of the Cherokee in eastern Tennessee and
the life and contributions of Sequoyah

Sequoyah Memorial
Route 1, Box 141
Sallisaw, OK 74955
918/775-2413
National Historic Landmark featuring the
cabin that Sequoyah built and lived in from
1829 until 1842

annuity
sum of money payable yearly or at another regular interval

bicameral
having two law-making groups

bribed
to have given money or gifts to influence a judgment or decision

calumet
highly ornamented ceremonial pipe used by Native Americans

cavalry
soldiers who ride horses into battle

ceded
to have given up, especially by treaty

civic
having to do with a city or the people who live in it

disability
condition that restricts what a person is able to do, usually because of an illness or injury or from a condition present from birth

encroaching
advancing beyond the usual or desirable limits

enlisted
to have voluntarily joined a branch of the military

guarantee
to promise that conditions will be met

improvised
made up out of what is available

Glossary

intruders
people who enter territory that is not theirs and without invitation

literacy
the ability to read and write

mediator
person who works with opposing sides in an argument in order to bring about an agreement

ritual
formal and customarily repeated act or series of acts

silversmith
person who makes goods of silver

stereotype
popularly held, often negative, impression of all members of an ethnic, religious, or other group

stockades
enclosures made of posts or logs set upright in the ground

syllabary
writing system in which each character represents a syllable of the language

tunic
shirt or jacket reaching to or just below the hips

venison
the flesh of a deer used as food

Chapter 2

Page 17, line 14: Stan Hoig. *Sequoyah: The Cherokee Genius*. Oklahoma City: Oklahoma Historical Society, 1995, p. 12.

Chapter 3

Page 25, line 7: Ibid., p. 46.

Chapter 4

Page 35, line 4: John P. Brown. *Old Frontiers: The Story of the Cherokee Indians from Earliest Times to the Date of Their Removal to the West, 1838*. Kingsport, Tenn.: Southern Publishers, 1938, pp. 480–481.

Page 36, line 2: Ibid., p. 481.

Page 37, line 2: Peter Collier. *When Shall They Rest? The Cherokees' Long Struggle with America*. New York: Holt, Rinehart and Winston, 1973, p. 50.

Page 37, line 22: "Sequoyah." Cherokee Nation. 17 Oct. 2006. www.cherokee. org/home.aspx?section=culture&culture=culinfo&cat=gV4q5zmQTuw=&ID=S WAHfDHmWs4=

Chapter 5

Page 44, line 7: Samuel Carter. *Cherokee Sunset: A Nation Betrayed: A Narrative of Travail and Triumph, Persecution and Exile*. Garden City, N.Y.: Doubleday, 1976, p. 61.

Page 49, line 1: *Sequoyah: The Cherokee Genius*, pp. 53–54.

Page 49, line 9: *Old Frontiers: The Story of the Cherokee Indians from Earliest Times to the Date of Their Removal to the West, 1838*, p. 483.

Chapter 6

Page 56, line 9: *Sequoyah: The Cherokee Genius*, pp. 46–47.

Chapter 7

Page 60, line 10: Ibid., p. 64.

Page 62, line 24: Ibid., pp. 67–68.

Page 65, line 7: Ibid., p. 71.

Chapter 8

Page 70, line 7: Earl Boyd Pierce and Rennard Strickland. *The Cherokee People*. Phoenix: Indian Tribal Series, 1973, p. 28.

Page 73, line 15: *Sequoyah: The Cherokee Genius*, p. 78.

Page 74, line 1: Grace Steele Woodward. *The Cherokees*. Norman: University of Oklahoma Press, 1988, p. 228.

Chapter 9

Page 79, line 20: *Sequoyah: The Cherokee Genius*, p. 88.

Bender, Margaret. *Signs of Cherokee Culture: Sequoyah's Syllabary in Eastern Cherokee Life.* Chapel Hill: University of North Carolina Press, 2002.

Brown, John P. *Old Frontiers: The Story of the Cherokee Indians from Earliest Times to the Date of Their Removal to the West, 1838.* Kingsport, Tenn.: Southern Publishers, Inc., 1938.

Carter, Samuel. *Cherokee Sunset: A Nation Betrayed: A Narrative of Travail and Triumph, Persecution and Exile.* Garden City, N.Y.: Doubleday, 1976.

Cassidy, James J., Jr., et al. *Through Indian Eyes: The Untold Story of Native American Peoples.* Pleasantville, N.Y.: Reader's Digest Association, 1995.

Collier, Peter. *When Shall They Rest? The Cherokees' Long Struggle with America.* New York: Holt, Rinehart and Winston, 1973.

Dockstader, Frederick J. *Great North American Indians: Profiles in Life and Leadership.* New York: Van Nostrand Reinhold Co., 1977.

Farb, Peter. *Man's Rise to Civilization.* New York: Avon Books, 1968.

Hirschfelder, Arlene, and Martha Kreipe de Montano. *The Native American Almanac: A Portrait of Native America Today.* New York: Macmillan General Reference, 1993.

Hoig, Stan. *Sequoyah: The Cherokee Genius.* Oklahoma City: Oklahoma Historical Society, 1995.

Hoig, Stan. *The Cherokees and Their Chiefs.* Fayetteville: University of Arkansas Press, 1998.

Mails, Thomas E. *The Cherokee People: The Story of the Cherokees from Earliest Origins to Contemporary Times.* New York: Marlowe & Company, 1996.

Malinowski, Sharon, ed. *Notable Native Americans.* Detroit: Gale Research, 1995.

Pierce, Earl Boyd, and Rennard Strickland. *The Cherokee People.* Phoenix: Indian Tribal Series, 1973.

Porter, C. Fayne. *Our Indian Heritage: Profiles of 12 Great Leaders.* Philadelphia: Chilton Books, 1964.

Starkey, Marion L. *The Cherokee Nation.* New York: Alfred A. Knopf, 1946.

Woodward, Grace Steele. *The Cherokees.* Norman: University of Oklahoma Press, 1988.

Teesee (son), 28, 30, 46–47, 77–81,
   85–86
Tennessee, 15, 28, 93
traditionalists, 25, 29
Trail of Tears, 71
Treaty of 1817, 28
Treaty of 1819, 29–30
Treaty of 1828, 61
Treaty of 1835, 69
Treaty of New Echota, 69
Treaty Party, 72–75
tribal identity, 13, 25, 65
Tsalagi (Cherokee language), 37
*Tsa'lagi' Tsu'llehisanun'hi (Cherokee
   Phoenix)*, 53–55
Turtle Fields, 35
Tuskegee, Tennessee, 15, 28, 30, 47

United States government, 23–24,
   26–28, 29–30, 55, 59–60, 67–68,
   69–70
U-ti-yu (possible wife), 29

Valley Settlements, 16
venison, 81

Washington, George, 17, 20
Waters, Michael (brother-in-law), 37,
   42
Waters, Sally (wife), 28, 36, 62, 91
Western Cherokee, 62–65, 72, 74
Wheeler, John F., 56
white settlers, 10, 23, 24–25, 31, 46,
   55, 59, 62, 67–68
Wichita Confederacy, 79
Wichita Indians, 79
Wild Potato Clan, 17
Willstown, Alabama, 31, 46–47
witchcraft, 10, 34
Wolf Clan, 17
Worm, the (friend), 77–81, 85–86
writing system, 10–12, 33–39, 41, 44,
   46, 48, 57
writing system test, 11–12, 42–43
Wurteh (mother), 16, 17

Roberta Basel began her literary career as an editor for a children's nonfiction publishing company. She became an author in 2004 and has written several children's books since then. In addition to writing, Roberta works as a freelance editor, proofreader, and fact-checker. She lives in southern Minnesota with her husband, Dustin, and their son, William.

Image Credits